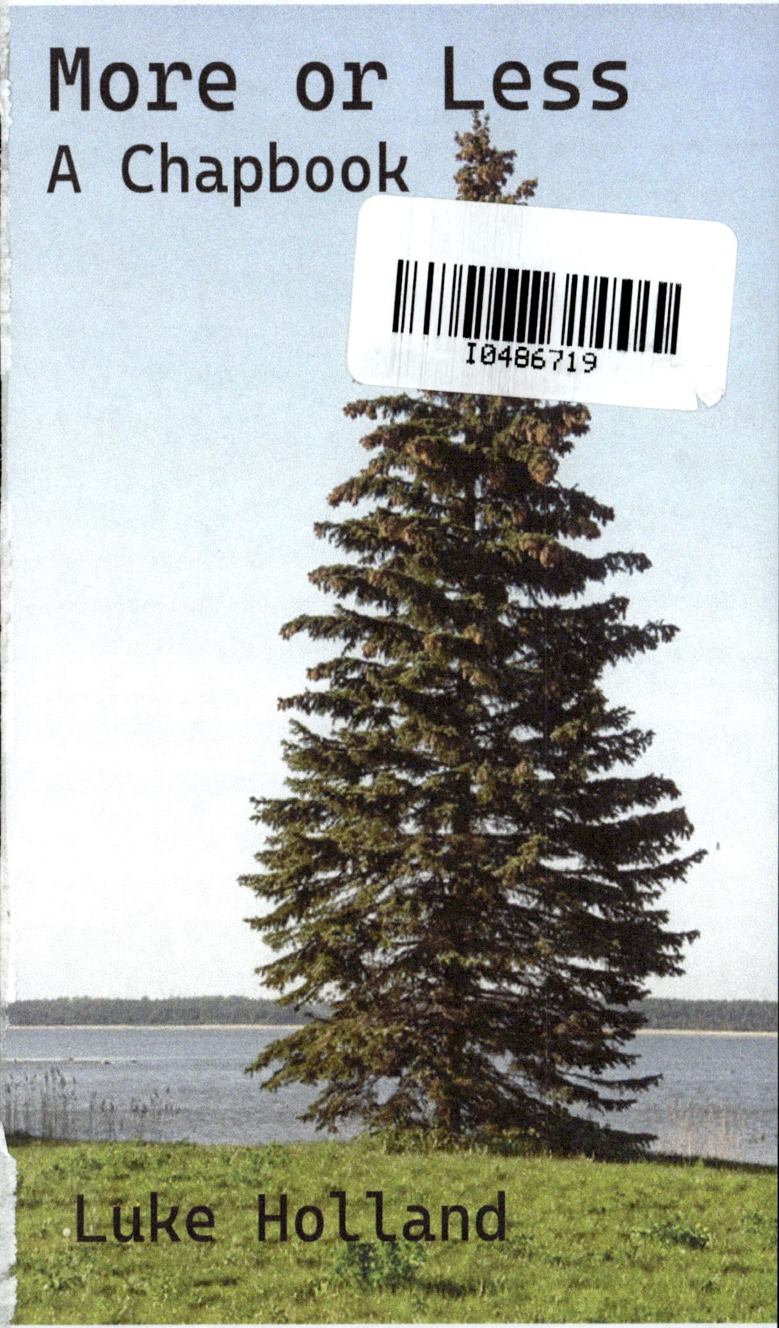

More or Less
A Chapbook

Luke Holland

LUKE HOLLAND

More or Less

A Chapbook by Luke Holland

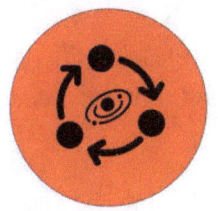

First published by Arcturus Publishing 2022

Copyright © 2022 by Luke Holland

This novel is entirely a work of fiction. The names,
characters and incidents portrayed in it are the
work of the author's imagination. Any resemblance
to actual persons, living or dead, events or localities
is entirely coincidental.

First edition

ISBN: 978-1-387-42527-3

This book was professionally typeset on Reedsy.
Find out more at reedsy.com

For Caiden

Contents

I   Death Stuff

Behind Death   3
The Darkless Night   11
Life   14

II   Science Fiction

Distances May Vary   29
The Stars   38
March 20th 2085   40

About the Author   52
Also by Luke Holland   53

I

Death Stuff

Short Stories and Poems that relate to the unavoidable movement of time and the inevitable arrival of death

Behind Death...................Short Story; Aug 17, 2022
The Darkless Night................Vendetta; Nov 6, 2022
Life....................................Short Story; Aug 29, 2022

Behind Death

I remember when I died, it was a relatively indifferent death. That is, it wasn't under extremely unique circumstances not that it wasn't unexpected. At first I felt my whole body jerk upwards and everything was white, the whole world appearing the same and infinite.

"What happened?" I asked the void, however, there was no response.

"Hello?" I shouted again, this time with slight panic.

"You died," said a jolly voice from the white, sounding almost pleased with my demise. I had plenty of questions but none of them seemed particularly pressing. I had technically spent my whole life preparing for this moment expecting it to be some major and surprising event, but this didn't feel that way at all.

"Where am I?" I asked again.

"Questions as always," the voice said. "You always were the curious type." The voice was a light one. A very joyful and pleasant voice that sounded almost inhumane in a kind way.

Suddenly a man appeared in the void standing calmly and staring at me. He wore a bright white suit, a suit that was just as white as the fog he stood in front of. Or was he sitting? His form was hard to describe, yet incredibly welcoming. Unique yet familiar.

"Who are you," I asked again.

"Michael ," He said quickly, his eyes bright and warm. "I'm your angel,"

I gave him a confused look which he responded to with one of his own.

"Oh right," he said, smacking his head. "You don't remember me."

"We've met?" I asked.

"Oh, yes many times," he said with a smile. "I suppose if we stayed here long enough your memories would return," he said looking around. "But there's really no point, I mean the second they got back they'd need to be taken away, but anyway the real reason I called you here was because something happened." He said quickly.

"What?" I asked.

Michael looked sad for a moment and then looked up. "You died."

"Yeah, you already made that joke. Anyway, what is this? A prank show?"

I said walking away and turning my attention back to the wide white world.

"This isn't a prank show," Michael said. "Here!" He shouted with excitement. "I'll prove it to you." Suddenly he jumped in the air. Much higher than any normal person would be able to, before landing on what was an invisible platform floating above the glowing ground. Then he looked back at me with a smug look in his eye like he had bested me, but I walked away.

"Where are you going," He asked as I left.

"Looking for a way out," I responded.

"I'm afraid that doesn't exist." He yelled.

"Maybe not for you," I shouted back.

"What's that supposed to mean," He asked appearing out of nothing directly beside me.

"OK, first that's not cool, ever heard of personal space."

"Sorry," he said stepping back shamefully.

"And second off this is a dream."

"A dream?" Michael questioned looking particularly annoyed. "And what does that make me."

"A person in my dream?" I guessed dismissively as I began to walk again. "Soon, I'll wake up and forget about all this."

"Oh, I'll make sure of that," Michael said quickly following me.

"You know maybe if you'd shown a little more

respect for others you wouldn't be here right now."
"I'm sure you're right," I answered again as I laid down on the glowing ground which did feel quite warm.

"You know I was starting to feel sorry for you,"

"How so," I asked placing my elbow over my eyes in an attempt to block out the never-ending light and this seemingly never-ending conversation.

"Well, you died pretty early,"

"I'm sure I-"

Then something unusual happened. It was almost like my brain had found something hidden away in its attic, an old memory of sorts. A Truck I remembered, a truck was looking at me and a loud horn was blaring. Of course, I tried not to let it be known that this had just happened but Michael seemed to know immediately, in fact Michael seemed to know before me.

"It's coming back isn't it,"

"I don't know what you're talking about."

"It's around this time that bits of old memories start to reform and judging by that stark look on your face I'd say it just happened to you. You still think this is all a dream?" Michael was now standing over me, his white suit nearly blinding me, his eyebrows stern and sharp.

"I don't have any evidence to convince me otherwise," I said with a slight chuckle.

"You're really gonna make me do it again uh?" He said, with a slight grin on his face. "You know I thought this time was going to be different, but I guess old habits die hard." Michael began to raise his hand and as it went up so did I. "Have it your way then." He said with a smile.

"Now wait, a second," I said trying to regain my footing, but it was too late, Michael had made up his mind and I was about to find out what a mistake it was.

The last thing I clearly remember was Michael slamming his hand down as the ground seemed to shatter beneath the world of white. The light now appeared like a star above what was now a pitch black void of nothingness. I fell uncontrollably through nothingness as my brain and mind seemed to melt into a soup.

Then it happened again. The truck was back and this time it was closer, its horn still blaring and brakes screeching.

"Michael!" I shouted but this time Michael didn't appear rather he simply spoke.

"Now you want me," His authoritative voice echoed throughout the shapeless nothing.

I knew I was falling, only because of the world of light. Its star becoming smaller and smaller, dimmer and dimmer.

"OK," I said with a heavy breath. "I believe you.

I am dead, but that doesn't make heights any less terrifying." I closed my eyes almost on the verge of tears when suddenly I saw warmth bleed through my eyelids. Looking down I saw another plane of infinite light, a plane that was not there 20 seconds ago. I braced for impact as I slammed into the floor which to my surprise didn't hurt a bit.

"I know," Michael said with a smile as he stood over top of my cowering self. "But it's still fun to watch."

"So, you believe me now uh?"

"I saw the truck again," I said.

"I thought you would. Now, what do you say I show you the way out of here?" He said, helping me to my feet.

"I'd like that," I said still shaking from my fall.

"You never let me explain why I brought you here."

"You brought me here, cause I'm dead."

"Not technically," he said, glancing at a white watch. "But you're getting pretty close. I save you at the last second."

"Why, I thought you were supposed to let events play out. Ya know free will and all."

"Us angels are given a little more leeway than you'd think, but I care about you, maybe a little more than most angels," Michael said, gesturing me forward as we both began to walk. "But I do think I got the best assignment and though sometimes you drive me and others crazy and yourself crazy I find you always come around. Plus we get better commissions the longer you live,"

Michael and I both laughed as we walked before he said.

"What do ya say we get you back to that life of yours," Michael asked.

"You can do that?" I asked.

"If you want to, I don't want to take your life away so fast."

Michael raised his hand again and just as before I floated up along with it.

"Not this again," I shouted with concern.

"Don't worry," Michael said. "The second time is always faster."

His hand slammed to the ground and instantly I found myself sitting in a car, my car, and sure enough directly in front of me was a skidding semi. Though it wasn't moving, and neither was I. Then Michael appeared floating outside the windshield waving with a big grin on his face.

"Alright," he said, his voice muffled through the windshield. "When I say go, jerk the wheel to the right. You ready?" He asked with eyes of eagerness.

I nodded firmly and Michael snapped his fingers. The truck unfroze and the world returned to full speed as I spun the wheel to the right and the truck's horn blared.

"That was a close one," I gasped as I passed it. "Thanks, Michael," I smiled as I continued driving, and Michael continued flying beside me with big bold thumbs up. Suddenly a beep was heard from the outside.

"I'll see you again, right?"

"I'm counting on you getting in a couple more pickles," he said.

"Don't hesitate to drop me again," I laughed. "I'll probably deserve it."

"No problem,"

"See you on the other side," I yelled.

"I already have," Michael said snapping his fingers.

The Darkless Night

Time is a cruel mistress
She preys on the naive youth
All run from her inescapable grasp
Death is her only true husband

She draws you in to her false cold embrace
Her eyes and face so dead yet inviting
She'll show you love before stabbing your heart
Time is a cruel mistress

She looks at life with a silent hatred
Her fist clenching in anger at its sight
You take it for granted but then its gone
She preys on the naive youth

She waits patiently rather then running
She doesn't waste herself on sorry lives
Not now but soon she'll have you too
All run from her inescapable grasp

Then its over as quick as it begun
She goes to her home with a sack of souls
He is the only master she will serve
Death is her only true husband

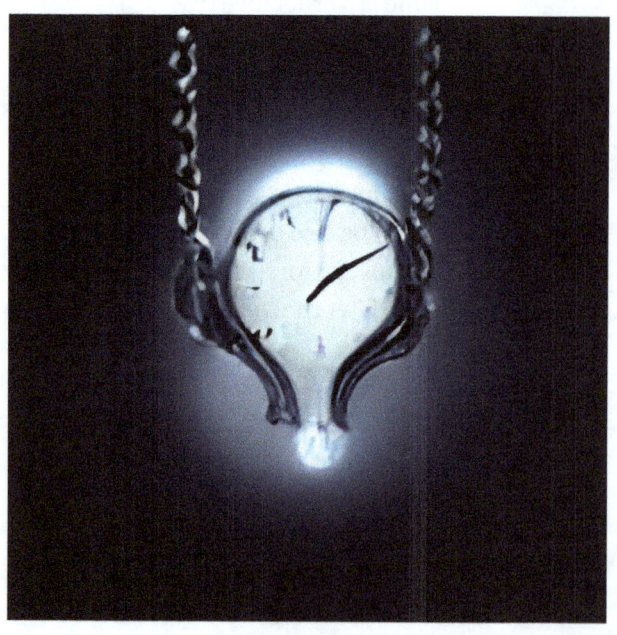

Life is a wonderful bride
A cavern full of hidden joy
Its looks at hardships with hope
Glancing at the couple with eyes of light and love

She rages at the sight of them leaving
Watching as they walk to meet their new partner
Though she still holds onto them they have let go of
her
Life is a wonderful bride

At first it appears dark even disgusting
But upon further investigation they find it's treasure
Reaching inside the darkness to pull out something
better
A cavern full of hidden joy

Her husband wipes away her eternal tears
As people laugh at the sight of a new day
She cries not giving them a promise of tomorrow
It looks at hardships with hope

Death then makes a promise of his own
Ensuring his bride he'll make them suffer
But even his power means nothing against the
darkless night
Glancing at the couple with eyes of light and love

Life

It all started on a relatively cold, hot day. The day itself however was not cold in the slightest rather it was warm, yet the atmosphere seemed to freeze in my presence. I was walking to the hospital along the sidewalk wearing a t-shirt and shorts on what was supposed to be a 100-degree day, but I was shivering. The people I passed stared at me, some with shock and some with concern, but I didn't pay much attention. A mother put herself in between her children and me. I couldn't really blame her. I'd probably stay away from someone who was freezing in August too. I continued my journey alone, teeth chattering as I stepped inside the hospital waiting room.

"Oh my," the receptionist gasped in a southern voice. "Honey, you alright?"

I looked up from my seat and took my head out of my hands.

"We need a bed in waiting room 5," she said into a microphone.

"What happened to you?" She asked as she felt my forehead.

"I d-don't know." I stuttered. "I just want to see my grandpa."

"You sure you're alright sugar?"

I nodded weakly, and after lowering her eyebrows she led me to my grandpa's room.

We walked through the hallways as I continued freezing. Getting occasional glances from the woman who I reassured with some half smiles.

After about five minutes of walking, we arrived. A solitary door at the end of an infinite hall.

"How was he last night?" I asked.

"Um," She paused. "I'm going to go get the doctor." Though something told me the doctor wasn't the only one who knew how my grandfather was doing. I walked into the room and for the first time all day, the environment was as cold as I.

"Hey, Grandpa," I said, walking into the room and sitting down beside the sleeping man. His breath was heavy and his eyes were closed in a forceful way. Hundreds of tubes ran up and down his face as his hands lay crossed on his chest.

"How'd you sleep?" His eyes slowly opened and his heavy breathing paused for a sigh.

"My time is almost up." He said in a cold voice.

"Why would you say that?" I responded with slight anger.

"I can see the end," He said again weakly, staring at the ceiling.

"The end of what?" I asked, already knowing the answer.

"The end of my burden, and with it-" He turned towards me, his eyes dim and sunken. "The beginning of yours."

"What are you talking about? What burden?"

"The burden of life," He said calmly. "And the burden of who it belongs to." Now he was *really* freaking me out.

"Here," he said with a cough. "Take this, I've carried it for too long." He then placed in my hand a necklace, a necklace that seemed to be way older than me or my grandpa. On the black and white chain was a stone of faint color. It looked like a rock slightly larger than marble with a black and white half in the center.

"What is this?" I asked, holding it up to the light, then as it glimmered I felt something warm, something alive.

"A gift, and a curse," He said. "Goodbye, Adam. I know you'll do good." His hand went slack in mine. My mind screamed for a doctor but my lips didn't move, the machines he was hooked up to began to beep and the heart rate died. Then I left feeling sad, guilty, and cold.

I walked along the street and this time I stayed

away from people. My strides got longer as a walk became a jog and a jog became a sprint, until I was flying towards my house with tears in my eyes. As I ran people parted ways clearly sensing I was upset. Then it happened. A voice spoke to me from somewhere unexpected: The necklace that was now glowing white spoke in a very audible and tangible way.

"Give Life," It said in a heavenly voice. "Give Life." I then did the only thing I could think to do. I placed the necklace around my neck and waited for something unexpected to happen and I did not have to wait long. Soon after wearing the necklace and a few more blocks, a semi-truck and a sedan were in opposite lanes of traffic. Then the sedan began to swerve and before I knew it a very unmatched collision was seconds away. I knew the driver of the car would die and normally I would have waited until after to help them, but the necklace had other plans. "Do you want him to live?" I heard from somewhere inside my mind.

"Yes?" I responded with a question.

"I need a firm answer." Its voice was heavenly, unearthly, and pure. It sounded like an angel, but I could also hear another voice behind it. The opposite of its goodness and love and while they seemed to be different I could tell that in at least some ways they were the same.

"Well, hurry up," it said with holy anger.

"I want the driver to live," I shouted aloud. Suddenly the car jerked away and got out of there with nothing more than a few honks of a horn.

"What was that?" I asked.

"You," said the voice. "Your desire and my power saved that man's life."

"Who are you?" I asked.

"A friend," It said. "At least for now."

I ran inside my house and raced up to my room, ignoring my parents before slamming the door behind me and later falling asleep from pure exhaustion. I awoke sometime later to my mom who seemed to know exactly what I had seen.

"Are you OK honey?" She asked.

"Yeah I uh," I said, still unaware of what was happening. "No, I am not OK. Grandpa-your dad's dead." I said frankly.

My mom sighed with tired eyes as she took a seat in my computer chair.

"I know," she said. "He's been dead for a while. Breathing, but dead."

"He gave me this before he died," I explained holding up the necklace which was now completely black. "Is this some kind of heirloom?"

"Kind of," She said backing away slightly. "Why don't you get dressed and we can talk some more? Don't worry about going to school today, you'll have enough questions as is." Before I could ask what she meant she got up and left, walking slowly down the stairs.

I walked downstairs after getting dressed and was at least somewhat relieved that I didn't have to go to school, but something about how she said it made me a little uncomfortable.

"What did you do after he gave this to you," She asked.

"I ran home."

"Nothing else?" My mom asked with raised eyebrows.

"Well, there was a truck." My mom let out a sigh. "Then there was a voice and it asked me if I wanted the driver to live," My mom's face grew tight with anxiety as I continued. "And I said yes." My mom sighed again.

"What?" I asked as I played with my hands on the table.

"Nothing, but don't do that again."

"Why not it's just some stupid coincidence."

"No, it's not."

"There is a gift in our family, and it comes from my side. Every male child is born with the ability to save anyone's life no matter what state it may be in."

"Well, that's awesome," I said, half sarcastic.

"Yes, it is." My mom laughed a little. "But it comes at a cost. Nothing is free in life. Not even life itself.

19

Every time you save someone's life, someone else will die." This clearly bore weight in my mother's words. Enough weight that I could tell she was serious.

"So someone died right after I saved the driver?" I asked with shock.

"No, not immediately but while you were sleeping your 'other self' went out and killed someone."

"My other self-killed someone? I would never kill someone," I said with shock

"No, I know you wouldn't but a part of you did."

"So I, don't save anyone else."

"That's easier said than done." My mom pointed . "My dad said he would do the same thing, but it's much harder to do that when you know you could save someone."

"Who did I kill?"

"I'm not sure, normally it's someone you have anger towards, eventually you'll be able to tell who will die next."

"So that's why Grandpa never came to family gatherings."

My mom nodded. "He didn't want to get mad at anyone."

"Can I go to school,"

"You sure?"

"Yeah," I needed some space away from my family and school felt like the only place where I could at least sort of be myself.

I went upstairs and grabbed my backpack. Then right before I closed the door, I threw the necklace on the bed trying to forget whatever "power" I had been given.

The walk to the school itself was a stressful one. You never really notice how dangerous everything is. A stop sign could impale someone, a fence could slice someone's vein. I doubted someone would get a lung disease from evaporating crosswalk paint, but I wasn't taking any chances. Anytime I encountered one of these objects I ran as far and as fast away as I could manage.

Then I made it to school, 2 hours late but I made it.

"Why are you late?" The principal asked.

"It's a long story,"

"Well, I don't have a lot of time," She responded. "Hurry along now, we will discuss this later."

The principal was the least of my concerns when you hold life and death in your hands you really reset your priorities.

I arrived at my 4th-period class and after my scolding by the teacher was told that I could sit down. I sat in my seat which to my surprise was right next to Thomas Lance, an old friend of mine.

"Why are you so late?"

"You don't want to know?" I assured him with dread.

"Maybe I don't but I do like that new necklace of yours."

Those words made my spine cold and looking down, I found it. The same disgusting necklace I had been given not even a day ago.

"Ah crap," I said with eyes raised to heaven.

"What, it's kind of cool."

"Not from where I'm sitting."

"Could you guys stop talking," said a small voice from behind us.

Claire was a girl no one really hung out with, and Thomas and I only sat near her because we felt bad.

"I'm sorry," she said with shame. "I'm just trying to listen."

"Yeah, sure thing," Thomas said kindly.

Claire kept staring at me for a while longer until I stared back, and her eye instantly snapped back to the whiteboard.

Then as if on cue Thomas turned back around and a piece of metal on his desk cut his wrist, This wasn't a bad cut, nothing fatal but it was still a cut and Thomas made it known that it hurt.

"Damn," he said with surprise as blood dripped down his arm.

"Here let me help you," I said, but immediately I knew I'd made a mistake. I felt the power, my power leave the necklace as it glowed a slight shade of white. Immediately Thomas's arm was healed and my stomach dropped.

"Oh no," I shouted like a lunatic.

"Whoa," Thomas responded as his arm stitched itself up. "What did you do,"

"I killed someone." I knew I had done it I just knew it.

"What are you talking about?" He asked with concern.

"Just come talk to me at lunch,"

Thomas met with me after class behind the gym, and it was there that his mind was forever blown and his trust in me was shattered.

"You mean you can heal or save anyone?" he asked with widened eyes, to which I nodded painfully.

"But every time I do someone dies,"

"Oh yeah, I forgot about that part. So when you healed me just now someone died."

"Not yet, but whenever I fall asleep my "other self" goes and kills someone."

"Quite grim," Thomas plainly said.

"Yeah, tell me about it."

"Well just don't help anybody ever again."

"Well, then I'd look like a complete jerk."

"I see your point."

"Well, don't you go getting mad at me now," he said. "I don't want to be the next one on the chopping block."

"Don't worry, your the last person I'd kill,"

"Kind of sounds weird like that, but thanks I guess."

"Don't mention it."

We went our separate ways; that night was the worst one of my life. I knew if I slept someone would die. So I bought and drank as many energy drinks as I could muster.

I stood up in the corner of my room in order not to lie down, all the while the necklace softly whispered its desires in my head.

"Just lay down for a moment," It said with its snake-like voice.

"You won't even notice us," It said again.

Eventually, however, I overcame these suggestions barely holding it together long enough to see the dawn. and it worked that night I did not fall asleep and after what seemed like an eternity the sun finally came up. The next day at school I went to class as tired as could be with what was probably my hundredth energy drink in my hand.

"Dude, you look terrible," Thomas said as he walked into class.

"Well, if I looked better someone would be dead." Thomas gulped with what I think was a touch of fear seeing me a little on edge.

"Excuse me," My teacher said as I walked in. "No drinks allowed."

"Uh, right?" I barely said with a conscience. "But,

I'm really thirsty." but before I could make any stronger arguments like I don't know, that fact that someone's life was literally on the line. She snatched the can right out of my hand and threw it in the trash can. Now I was mad. She had just doomed someone's life and I was going to feel the guilt.

"Just close your eyes," The necklace said.

"Just, go with it man you can't stay awake forever." Thomas was right and the minute I realized the awful truth I lost the ability to fight it.

"That's it," The voice said as I lay my head on my desk. "Close those weary EYES,"

Then it happened immediately and suddenly.

"I hadn't even noticed I had fallen asleep when my teacher dropped dead in front of her class.

"HOLY-"

The class went crazy, as a class should when their teacher suddenly turns into a corpse.

Claire walked in to take her seat, passing the body which the other students were clearly freaking out about.

"Come with me," she said sternly, her quiet voice replaced by one of confidence and authority. "You've got a lot to learn." Then I noticed the small black and white gem hanging around her neck.

II

Science Fiction

These are short stories about anything from teleportation to entire realities being lies and the occasional poem about stars and black holes.

Distances may Vary...........................Short Story, Oct 2022

The Stars..........................Inventive Form Poem, Nov 2022

March 2085........................Dystopian Short Story, Sep 2022

Distances May Vary

I was working in the factory late at night as I often do. It was a great night, one filled with productivity and progress rather than that wasteful counterpart, what was it called again, oh yeah: sleep. Anyway, I had just finished cleaning up and was about to head out for the night when I heard a noise from the back of the warehouse. Now this factory was never particularly quiet with all the machines and robots; something always seemed to be moving even when no one was around. However this sound was different, it seemed to be almost intentional like someone had done it on purpose and with deliberate action. Whether or not it was good, I still have yet to find out. Curious as a cat, I let the door close as I turned around, and walked back through the lab. Up the stairs and into what some would describe as mankind's greatest invention. The reactor is an interesting thing that no one fully understood, not even the inventor. It seemed that the reactor itself was almost alive, constantly twirling its thumbs with electromagnetic plasma that generated enormous amounts of power and energy. I watched as the door that guarded it flashed and hummed. No one was allowed inside the inner room without special authorization and especially after hours.

I had just broken one rule.

Its red light flashed and flickered from inside its glass prison as I slowly stepped inside. Swirling around the bright blue core like a swarm of electrified locusts. Then I saw it, a crack in the glass, not a large one but a crack nonetheless. I placed my hand on the crack and felt a warm energy churning inside. A crack in the glass required an immediate evacuation and a shutdown of the reactor itself, but I didn't sound an alarm or alert anyone to its presence.

I had now broken two rules.

It almost called me, not that it could, but I still felt something inside. Something powerful. My lab coat rustled around as the red-hot energy began to seep through the crack. I placed my hand on the crack again and this time didn't stop at the glass. Cutting my hand on the sharp edges as blood slowly dripped down my fingers dropping down on the metal floor of the core. The power from the still-swirling matter was almost overwhelming. Until—.

I had now broken three rules.

All at once, the electrified energy rushed through my hand. It felt as though the sun's power itself had entered my body and some would say it had. My lab coat buttons began to melt and my shoes welded themselves to the floor. I tried to pull my hand out of the glass but it was stuck, almost like the energy was pulling me further in. The glass exploded all around me and now there was nothing to keep me contained, but I still found it impossible to leave. Then as quick as it had begun, it stopped. The reactor was empty, alarms were blaring and I had one hell of a headache. I rushed out the door leaving my shoes and coat behind as I ran towards my car. I sat in the driver's seat for what felt like an hour, but it had been only a couple of seconds. I checked my car's clock: 11:59 pm. and slowly drove home.

Opening the door to my house was a thing I had done so much I had never really thought about, but this time it was even easier. I didn't have to do it. I stepped out of my car onto what was the driveway, but then as my feet touched what should have been asphalt, I felt carpet, MY carpet. Upon looking up again, I saw my living room, my car vanishing into nothingness as I now stood in my own house scared straight. I ran back outside, and my car was exactly where I had parked it.

"This dream was weirder than I thought," I said to myself as I stepped back inside. Sleep was especially confusing; I distinctly remember stepping out of the shower when all of a sudden I found myself lying in bed dressed in pajamas and all. Almost as if someone had decided to change the scene of a movie. I looked around but everything seemed normal, and I went to bed with the belief that I was just extremely tired. I woke up and looked around suspiciously waiting for the world to change.

"I knew I was crazy," I mumbled under my breath as I got out of bed and threw the sheets to the end of the bed. I stepped on the ground and found myself standing in my driveway, clothed in a black suit, a perfectly tied tie wrapped around my neck, and a briefcase in my hand. I also noticed how I was reaching for the car door with my hand.

"Ok," I sighed with nervousness as I slowly got in the car and reached for the shifter, anxious about where I would find myself next. I rushed to my lab where I found police and fire engines waiting in the parking lot. I got out of my car to inspect the trouble.

"You're late!" John shouted as I stepped on the ground which thankfully remained static. John is one of my oldest friends and has also been known to work late nights.

"Wouldn't matter," I said pointing to the lab with my hand on a cup of coffee.

John chuckled and walked over to me.

"Yeah, I've been meaning to talk to you about that,"

"You notice anything strange last night with the reactor?"

"The reactor? " I lied with a tinge of nervousness behind my words.

"Yeah," John questioned. "The whole system went down and there was no alarm."

"You got anything for me?" He asked as he began to lean on the chain link fence that surrounded the lab.

"No," I said with about 50% confidence. "No, I don't know what happened."

"All right," John said with a sigh. "But the boss isn't going like this."

The boss did not like this.

"WHAT IN THE HELL OPERATION DO YOU THINK WE ARE RUNNING HERE!!!" He screamed in the parking lot. He was a large man, going bald, and had a loud gluttonous voice. He was so comical when he yelled, we all found it hard not to snicker, me included.

He looked at me with sharp round eyes and stopped his sentence.

"You think this is funny boy?" He yelled, breathing heavily down my neck.

"No sir," I said quietly.

"We have just lost what could quite possibly be the most prized scientific discovery this world has ever seen and yet we're standing out here laughing." We all giggled from his anger and that was enough to make him snap, and I mean really snap.

"I HAD IT WITH YOU GUYS," He screamed, and just as he finished a bird landed on his head and I burst out laughing.

Then my boss did something extreme for even him. He stepped forward towards me and with a little hop and dance from his lab coat swung his fat fist square at my nose. I closed my eyes and placed my arms in front of my face, but I didn't feel an impact. For the smallest moment I believed I was dead, but then I heard the gasp from my coworkers and a quiet exchange of shock between them. I opened my eyes and found that I was now behind my boss staring at the place I once was.

My boss missed his punch and stared at his fist then at me, and smirked.

"You've made 2 mistakes now boy." My boss said as he lunged at me again, but just as before the world seemed to shift and I was somewhere new. Jumping around the parking lot as my boss who seemed relatively unfazed by the fact that I was teleporting in front of his eyes. My coworkers, on the other hand, were not, pulling out phones to either call the police, physic center, or to simply take a video.

"How are you doing that," John asked as my boss began to run out of breath.

"I don't know," I said as I continued to uncontrollably melt the very fabric of space. As I was talking to John my boss snuck up behind me and this time, he made contact. I'm not really sure how he hit me but then again, I wasn't sure of a lot of stuff back then. His fist hit my neck and I was launched across the parking lot. Now I'm not a very strong person and would never *try* to pick a fight with my boss but in my defense, he punched first, and at this point (if you really squinted) what I was about to do was self-defense.

I slowly got up from my boss' crushing blow and let my newfound power flow freely, no longer letting it just wander around aimlessly. Now I was channeling it at someone and that someone happened to be my boss who was currently charging at me. I jumped in the air and brought my fist down towards him then my boss did something unexpected: *he* teleported, vanishing into nothingness in front of my eyes, and reappearing instantly in my peripheral vision. My fist struck the solid asphalt and my hand exploded in pain.

"How?" My brain seemed to say.

"This is much bigger than you think," My boss said with a grin, his hands glowing with power as he slowly walked towards me and I awaited my death.

What happened next was one of the weirdest and yet most real moments I had ever had in my entire life. All I can remember is the simmering heat of the sun on my back and the grim look on my boss's face as his fist made its lethal descent. It was one of those moments where you feel death touch your shoulder as your whole world begins to wither up and die at that very moment.

Then as I felt death pick me up and my body evaporates, I saw John out of the corner of my eye, throwing something through the air. I didn't even know what it was, yet I could see salvation in it. It landed with a clank beside me, and I saw what appeared to be a small metal syringe.

I rolled to the side, my body filling itself with what was most likely its last rush of adrenaline. I felt the wind of a fist and the sound of thunder whiz by my ear as I reached the syringe and jabbed it as far and as hard as I could into my boss's ankle.

My boss twitched a little in his eye and fell flat on his back. A familiar cold red plasma filling the syringe.

"Dude," John said, running over, "We gotta talk."

The Stars

Humanity reaches for the Stars
just as all civilizations must
the step is needed but way is far

making it difficult to adjust
though the first step is already made
the second one requires more trust

as our new futures groundwork is laid
why you might ask do we have to leave
because there is nothing if we stayed

lookup for we are on a new eve
one we must look to with it A New Hope
and New Horizons we have to cleave

please let go my child you will cope
for this future is not mine but ours
we must go to the stars, our final Hope

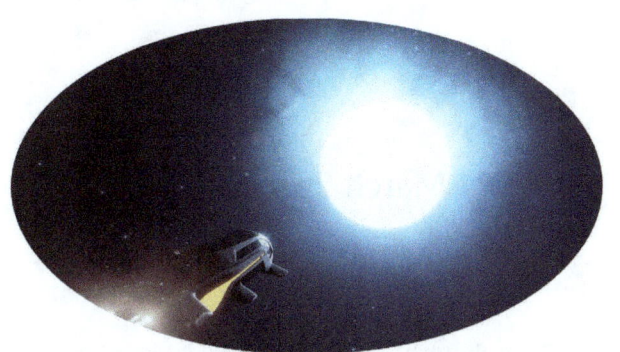

Photo taken by Luke Holland in Elite Dangerous
Horizons

March 20th 2085

March 20th, 2085 was a typical day for most people, but not for me. You see it was my day, a day that could never seem to get here fast enough, but this year it was especially true. This year was my 14th birthday. A 14th birthday is a particular time in a boy's life because it is when he receives his first reality. A boy's first reality is often filled with superheroes or magic but mine, I was going to make mine something really special, I just didn't know what yet.

"How long does it take?" I asked my dad as I joyfully skipped to the store.

"Not long," He responded.

"But will it hurt?"

"Mine didn't,"

We continued to walk down the street, carefully avoiding any cracks or crevices in the concrete as we stepped.

"I don't like cracks in the concrete," I said as we walked some more.

"Well, you'll be through with them forever in a moment," My dad responded with a soft smile.

"What've you gotten rid of?" I asked my dad.

"Thunder," My dad answered quickly. "Never was fond of violent noises,"

"Anything else,"

"Nothing that concerns you, after all this isn't my special day," He chuckled.

We finally made it to the store after what felt like an eternity of skipping and crack avoidance.

The reality store was one of the largest stores in the city and always seemed to be packed full of customers.

We walked inside and it felt like seeing color for the first time. I had always peeked my head in the window of the store but this was the first time I had ever really been allowed inside. No one under 14 was allowed in the store let alone create their pocket universe. The store was alive with imagination and fun, nothing sad or dreary in sight, only smiles and happiness. New children created their very first world as they laughed and played with invisible unicorns and superheroes that now existed somewhere beyond their imagination.

"My my Mr. Brown," The store manager said, rushing up to us with his crazy eyes and a wide smile. "Is it that day already?" I nodded with glee and my dad concurred. Everyone in town knew the store owner, he was bright and bold, with a personality that seemed to be churning with the very essence of imagination. His name was Reli, some people called him Relish for fun but most people called him by his more formal name of Mr. Breeze.

"Well, I suppose we better get started right away," he responded, whisking me away toward the opposite end of the store. Mr. Breeze wore a light brisk suit that almost seemed to float in the wind and was one of the only people in town who consistently wore such clothing. We arrived at a door near the back of the store so that the once blusterous laughing and screaming of children was not a dull roar in the back of my mind. Reaching for his keys, Mr. Breeze began to fumble at the lock for a moment before landing on the correct key.

"Now then," He said, walking into the dark and musty room. "Where shall we begin?"

We began from the beginning, as neither one of us could come up with an alternative. The room's lights switched on and immediately I could tell this was not like any room I had been in before.

The room, while not being much wider than my initial blind estimate was certainly overwhelming when looked at from a different perspective. The long hallway ran down the light with drawers and cabinets crowing the walls with papers and metal shavings scattered around. Mr. Breeze did not waste any time and quickly began to look in all the drawers.

"How do you find the one?" I asked.

"Everyone is different," He said dismissively. "No two minds are alike, so why should two realities follow anything different?"

Mr. Breeze continued working his way around the hallway quickly peering into drawers before shutting them just as fast.

"How do you know when you'll find it?" I asked.

"Oh, I'll know," He said again as I began to loosely follow him in his search.

"A reality always reflects the desires of its owner and so too does the Owner reflect the values of the reality."

I was about to ask another question when Mr. Breeze exclaimed. "I found the one," He shouted with joy scrambling through the cabinet, throwing papers and pencils all around the room.

"This is the one," He said nearly exploding as he walked it over to me.

In his hand was a round spherical shape no bigger than a table tennis ball; its red shiny surface captured my attention immediately.

"Do you like it?" He asked.

"It's perfect," I said taking it in my hands.

"Well..." Mr. Breeze said.

"Well, what?"

"Well don't just stand there staring at it."

43

"Go on make your first reality." He said with eagerness. I held on tight to the ball and thought. Then I opened my eyes and in my hand where the ball had been was a perfect ice cream cone, overflowing with delight.

"How does it look," Mr. Breeze asked, almost immediately knowing what it was I was holding in my hand.

"Well, try some." He encouraged. I brought the cool treat to my lips and to my immense surprise and delight it did taste like ice cream.

"How is it?" He asked.

"Real," I said with glee.

"It is," I looked back to Mr. Breeze with confusion and a slight laugh.

"Well yeah I guess, but just for me right."

"So what?" He said cleaning up the mess he had made. "That's all that matters." He explained taking the ball from my hand, the magical ice cream slowly fading away.

"Mr. Breeze?" I asked as I rushed back to the cabinet.

"Yes?" He responded with his head buried deep within the cabinet as he searched for a tool.

"What if two people believe different things?"

"What do you mean?" He asked dismissively.

"Like if I think I'm holding ice cream but someone else thinks I'm holding a soda."

"Oh yeah," He said knowingly. "Happens all the time, each person just sees what they want to see."

"Oh," I said questionably. "Well, how much stuff can I change?"

"We start you guys out pretty small, but as you get better, we'll begin to move some of the initial restrictions until you have control of everything."

"You mean I could control everything," I asked in disbelief.

"Not could," Mr breeze said walking back over and placing the ball back in my hand the ice cream instantly reappeared. "Will,"

Mr. Breeze walked me back to my dad and after a quick exchange of words between the two and a swipe of a credit card we left the store.

"How'd it go?" My dad asked as we walked back.

"Awesome," I said. "Look at my ice cream," I held up the treat to my dad who responded with a laugh.

"I can't see it silly,"

"Oh, right,"

"Your reality and my reality are different."

"I guess but then how do we know whose right?"

"What do you mean?" My dad asked.

"Like, if I believe one thing and you believe something else then one person is right and another person is wrong."

"No one can be wrong son," My dad corrected. "That's the whole reason we invented these things."

Suddenly the cracks began to seal themselves as we walked, each one fusing until the sidewalk was one continuous concrete path. No longer did I have to consciously think about what I wanted to change, rather my subconscious mind made demands of its own.

"I know but someone is right,"

"I'm not sure what you're saying?" My dad asked.

"I just don't know what's real anymore," My dad's lower lip began to tighten, and clouds vanished instantly from the sky.

"Sure you do,"

"Not really, I mean whatever my reality is could be different than someone else's so whose right which reality is the truth," That word carried infinite weight as my dad and even some onlookers froze.

"Where did you learn that word," My dad said, clouds, cracks, and cones all returning to their original state.

"Reality?" I asked.

"No the other one," My dad looked as though it would explode right then and there.

"Truth?" My dad cringed and cowered in place.

"You must never say that word again,"

"Why not, it's just a word?"

"No, it is more than that,"

"What do you mean?"

"You don't remember, and it's a good thing you

don't. I couldn't imagine growing up in a time like that."

"What are you talking about?"

"Nothing," my dad said looking at bystanders who continued to stare.

"Let's go home, I'll explain everything there. Until then, not a word," I nodded silently and walked home in slight shame. I placed my hand on the cold metal ball that lay comfortably in my pocket and with a single thought corrected the world of everything wrong. The sky exploded with sunshine and rainbows. The grass grew flowers as large as trees, birds of all kinds came and sang the most beautiful songs, and then there was the house. My house was the most magnificent and gorgeous building I had ever seen, the path lined with orchids and daisies. A slight breeze blew petals of all colors around me and my dad as we walked up the steps to the door. Then everything changed as I reached for the doorknob and momentarily forgot where I was.

My house was not beautiful at all, rather it was quite broken. The once golden door was now rusted, the rust was hidden behind a thick green layer of mold and moss. The heavenly wood creaked with envy as my vision of our home completely faded out and the wooden floors returned to their monotone appearance.

"Come here son," my dad remarked, pulling out

a chair from our rustic dining table. Suddenly the memories of my life faded out, and though I hadn't forgotten them it was clear they had been pushed out for some time. Removed from my mind to make room for new and glorious ideas, only those new ideas were different. Not because they were better, but because they were lies.

"Dad, why don't we live in a nicer place?" I asked, placing the ball on the table, causing it to roll around anxiously.

"We do," he said with a slight tinge of confusion. "Ah," he said, reaching for the sphere and wrapping my palm around it. The same glorious fantasy sparked back to life. "There ya go," He said with a smile. "Now we live in whatever house you want." I looked around for a moment, the incredible images that lay in front of me singing and dancing with joy. The kitchen was glorious. the lights were shining with unmatched power, and the walls seemed to sing. However, it wasn't the same. Something was off, behind all of the singing, shining and glory was something dark and sinister about this new and beautiful world I had created. It was clear that what was in front of me was a lie. I pushed the ball back towards my dad and the room faded back to the truth, the gloomy truth, but it was real and that was something the lie didn't have.

"I can't do this," I said with a heavy breath.

"What are you talking about, sure you can," He rolled the ball back my way. "All you need to do is think," The ball reached me. I stared at it for what felt like a lifetime and in a certain sense I did.

In that cruel piece of shiny metal, I saw every lie and fib I had ever told. Then I saw all the lies I could create with the ball itself. My dad had become corrupted by this same device and if I didn't make the right choice it would do the same to me.

"Son, do you know what privilege you have," My dad remarked. "When I was your age everyone was fighting and arguing. It was ceaseless and endless they were looking for something that during that time made the world itself go round."

"What were you searching for?" I asked, my eyes widening with wonder.

"The same thing you are to never speak of again."

"Truth?" My dad loudly inhaled, a not-so-subtle reminder of the gravity of the word.

"Yes," He said with a large sigh. "They were look-ing for the_____" he explained, carefully omitting the word himself. "Now we don't have to worry about that thing ever again," I stared blankly at the table.

"Come on son," he said, "You've been waiting for this your whole life." Then silently and subtly. I got up from the table, set the ball in front of my dad, and began to walk towards the door.

"You're making a mistake!" He yelled as I reached

the door and placed my hand on the knob.

"Please son!" He yelled as I reached the porch. "Don't leave me!" Tears rolled slowly down his cheeks as he ran to stop me.

"Dad I can't live this lie with you anymore. It's unnatural."

"I know, I know but how am I supposed to leave this?" He said pointing back to the house that looked like it was about to collapse in on itself. I looked at the house then my dad, then I looked at his pocket. I reached inside and pulled out a blue ball that was slightly larger than my own. My dad grabbed my wrist as I began to take the ball away from him.

"Dad," I said with firm compassion, "you need to let go." His fist still felt like a grip of iron.

"I can't," he said. "Without my reality then I'm wrong, and I can't be wrong." His eyes were over-flowing dark pools as the water from within began to trickle down his face.

"You can't be right if you don't know what's wrong." I removed his hand from my wrist, my dad falling down inches away from the soon-to-be graveyard of his everything. I placed the ball on the ground and took one last look at my dad.

"Please," He begged as I raised my foot. "I don't like this!" He yelled again in desperation.

"Don't worry," I said. "You'll be through with it forever in a moment."

I put my foot down.

"NO!" He screamed in terror as the ball shattered into an infinite amount of dark blue pieces.

"You have no idea what you just did!" I stood there shocked as my dad continued to shout.

Suddenly a black ink came from the corpse of the sphere, covering everything in a beyond-midnight black.

"What the—," I said with confusion as the ink began to spread like paint. I backed away as it climbed trees and engulfed the sky until the only light came from reflections.

"Now you'll see the truth," My dad said as he also became surrounded by the liquid and faded into the void. A Tsunami of darkness roared behind me and engulfed the dimming sky. I looked around and saw nothing. The world was before me and my thoughts were as dead and cold as the world. March 19th, 2085 was a normal day for most people, but not for me.

About the Author

Luke Holland is currently 18 years old and lives in Tampa Florida with his family of seven. He has self published a novel and a novella in high school and middle school respectively. He currently spends his free time writing poetry and riding his boosted board as well as the occasionally poker game. His favorite subjects are Science and Math. And his favorite video games are but are certainly not limited to: Minecraft, Elite Dangerous, and Among Us. He also loves 80s music.

Also by Luke Holland

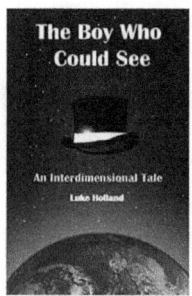

The Boy Who Could See
Other worlds exist beyond your own. Dimensions, universes, realities; call them what you wish, but I assure you that they are real. You might be confused right now, but that's good. I'd be concerned if you weren't. Matthew was also confused about the existence of these strange new worlds and the war that was about to be fought over them. Owen Hive's army is growing stronger by the minute and each time it does the dimensions themselves become darker as his grip on anti-matter and reality itself tightens. You might think to yourself "this doesn't make any sense?" But hey, a lot of stuff won't, well at least to you.